JUDGING THE POLICE

by Bryan Muth

authorHOUSE™

1663 LIBERTY DRIVE, SUITE 200
BLOOMINGTON, INDIANA 47403
(800) 839-8640
WWW.AUTHORHOUSE.COM

AuthorHouse™
1663 Liberty Drive, Suite 200
Bloomington, IN 47403
www.authorhouse.com
Phone: 1-800-839-8640

AuthorHouse™ *UK Ltd.*
500 Avebury Boulevard
Central Milton Keynes, MK9 2BE
www.authorhouse.co.uk
Phone: 08001974150

First published by AuthorHouse 3/29/2007

ISBN: 1-4208-8876-5 (sc)

Printed in the United States of America
Bloomington, Indiana

This book is printed on acid-free paper.

JUDGING THE POLICE

The post-Rodney King-era police officer is more tenuous and fearful of citizen complaint or prosecution than ever before in history. The "L" word (liability) is fast becoming the first concern of a cop, not public safety.

Officers are being reviewed through citizen groups, ad hoc committees, or civil juries whose members only yesterday told a police officer, "I wouldn't do your job for a million bucks."

Offenders as young as ten years old are trying to intimidate an officer from doing his job by demanding to talk to the officer's supervisor. Unfortunately, IT IS WORKING!

You are not as safe from crime as you would think, or as police administrators and politicians would like you to believe.

CONTENTS

DEDICATION

To my father, Andres S. Muth, who passed away in 1990 after serving with the Michigan State Police for more than twenty-six years, and an additional fourteen years with other law enforcement agencies. Dad, I'm sorry I sarcastically told you it was time for you to retire when you said to me, "Son, are you sure you want to do this job? The cops of the future will have to concern themselves with complaints, lawsuits, and in some cases, prosecution." Dad, you were RIGHT ON THE MONEY!

To the men and women of America who paid the ultimate sacrifice in service to their communities, and to their families, who sacrificed so much as well.

A PORTION OF THE SALES OF THIS BOOK WILL BE DONATED TO THE NATIONAL LAW ENFORCEMENT OFFICER MEMORIAL FUND MUSEUM TO OPEN IN LATE 2009.

Special Thanks:

K.S. Allbright   D. Chambers

W.R. Willm   H. Bullis   B. Bullis

T. Birr   L. Bolton   J. Tolan

C. Spiess   R. Driscoll

TO THESE OFFICERS AND THEIR FAMILIES

JASON WOLFE, 7215
EOW: 8-28-04

ERIC WHITE, 7275
EOW: 8-28-04

DON SCHULTZ, 4410
EOW: 5-12-04

DARROL YOOS, 3101
12-22-04

DAVID URIBE, 4276
EOW: 5-10-05

WE WILL NEVER FORGET

Andres Muth during early years as a Michigan State Trooper.
In the 1940s, troopers had to take a turn at
"fatigue" duty washing cars, etc. A certain
grievance for modern-day law enforcement.

INTRODUCTION

This book is designed as a "how-to" book for those who might find themselves sitting in judgment of a police officer after performance, or in some cases, non-performance of his duties.

I want you to be able to remove any and all emotions when rendering a decision on the incident. You will have plenty of time to decide whether the actions or inactions of the officer were correct. The officer had only seconds to choose a course of action. Your time is not limited. Juries, use-of-force boards, citizen review committees, and prosecutors are not under time restraints.

Each chapter has three sections: policy/procedure, actual cases, and scenarios. Try to put yourself in the officer's place when making the decision. You can't use the lack of training or experience as a defense, because if you are sitting on one of these panels in review of an officer, you are doing so as a layman. Only your opinion counts and will affect the officer's career and possibly determine his fate.

If you are doing the scenarios alone, then don't cheat. Make your decision and then read the results on the next page. If you are administering the scenarios to groups, follow this format.

PICK SOMEONE TO BE THE OFFICER. SEND TWO PERSONS OUT OF THE ROOM DURING THE SCENARIO. (They will act as the civil jury and criminal jury.)

THE CIVIL JURY WILL DECIDE WHETHER THE AGENCY/OFFICER MUST PAY AN AWARD TO THE PLAINTIFF.

THE CRIMINAL JURY DECIDES THE OFFICER'S FATE AND THUS HIS FREEDOM.

MARK THIS PAGE AND REFER TO IT DURING EACH SCENARIO.

PROLOGUE

I knew early on in life that I would go into some type of public service when I got older. I wasn't sure if it would be police work, but I knew I had to be active, needed, and not punch a clock every day.

I began in the business as a second person on an ambulance when I was only sixteen years old. Back then, there were no laws or rules governing ambulance personnel, although the employer I worked for did prefer that employees had a first aid class under their belt.

The ambulance service I worked for was operated by a funeral home. The funeral director also owned a furniture store, and the hotline also rang into the store. If an ambulance call came in, he would have to close the store, drive a couple of blocks to the funeral home, and get the ambulance. He would then have to come a few more blocks and pick me up, and we were underway.

It was probably a good five minutes or more before we were even on the way to the emergency. There were often allegations back then that funeral homes took their time getting to an emergency, because the funeral home made better money if the patient died. I can assure you that the ambulance folks I knew and worked with or for did everything they could back then to sustain life. The funeral business was never a factor.

Before deciding on law enforcement, I tried about everything in public service, as long as it had a flashing light on top of the vehicle. This included driving a snowplow for a while.

At one point, I was working full time during the day for a professional ambulance service and was a part-time police officer in a small village. I was paid $5.00 an hour.

I pinned on my first badge as a police officer only days after returning from the Viet Nam War. I was hooked after that. I felt I could make a difference in this career, serving the public best.

I did take a temporary break from law enforcement to go to work for General Motors as a plant protection specialist. Although we did some fire service and ambulance work, it was a glorified gate guard job and I hated it. After less than two years, I left GM and returned to the streets that I missed so much.

I came from a public service family. My father was a Michigan State Police officer for more than twenty-six years, and my grandfather retired from the Detroit Fire Department.

I thought about the fire service for a while, and even served on a volunteer force for a bit; however, I quickly learned that not only did I not like sitting around waiting for the bell to ring, I hated ladders and heights.

A police officer might find himself in high places now and then, to talk a suicidal person out of jumping, but those cases are few and far between. The officer can usually set his own space and distance for those cases.

When I first started in police work, I thought that most citizens appreciated and supported what we did, and back then, that usually was the case. Respect, if not fear, kept most offenders from resisting arrest. An officer could often affect an arrest by himself without a backup. Now, you need another officer or two just as a witness.

I used to love hearing my father's stories about his early years with the state police in 1941. Most law enforcement officers used motorcycles because they were much faster than the early cars. If it was necessary to transport a prisoner, the troops would flag down a passing motorist and have them transport the handcuffed prisoner to the nearest police station with the officer following.

In the 1970s, I was taking some law-enforcement-related classes at a community college when I had my first taste of mistrust of the police. The class was a driver safety program, made up largely of offenders who were court ordered into the class to avoid the fine or points on their license. When I signed up, I thought it was something different, but decided to stick it out and see what it was all about. I quickly learned that the folks in the class were not supporters of the police.

They all had a "not guilty" story and a criticism of the police. Even the instructor started off the course by asking the class why in the world anyone would want to be a police officer?

One answer stood out among all others. That answer came from an editor of a local newspaper, who found herself in the class obviously because the officer had a quota to fill. She said that "Cops became cops because of the power they have over the people." I had just returned from an unpopular war in Viet Nam and knew that the liberal media was anti anything government or authority, but this statement angered me. I was new to the police business, but I knew that I personally was not power-hungry; I just wanted to make a difference.

That power statement stuck with me the rest of my career, because I now know that the editor had much more power than I ever did or would have. The power of the pen is clearly mightier than the sword. I strongly believe that many a police officer has died from inactions because of what they feared would be written about them in tomorrow's headlines.

Although we are not yet in crisis, I believe we have a lot of problems coming for America's law enforcement community. Many agencies have already found themselves in recruiting dilemmas, with a shortage of QUALIFIED applicants. The agencies have to decide whether or not to lower their standards or to work short-handed and risk burning out the troops.

The biggest problem with recruitment, if not everything in life right now, is DRUGS. Most state certification boards do not allow for any recreational drug use in the applicant's past. When I began my law enforcement career, the use of marijuana was strictly forbidden. Now many agencies allow for pot use if you have not toked up in six months before the academy begins. I am proud to say I am one of the few who NEVER tried the funny tobacco.

Another problem with recruiting and retaining officers is the current military actions and wars going on around the world. Many of our military personnel fighting so bravely overseas came from the police ranks either through the national guard or reserves. Also many of these men and women on deployment had plans of joining a police agency when they got out of the service.

I have noticed in many of the news stories on those fallen heroes killed in action that they were planning law enforcement careers. The country lost dearly both in the war and in the law enforcement community.

Shortly before leaving Viet Nam in 1968, I read a notice by then-Secretary of Defense Robert S. McNamara (see Figure 1.A, 1.B) offering early outs of up to ninety days from the war if MEN would agree to join a police force in the United States. The war was depleting the ranks of domestic law enforcement.

In the 1960s, women in police work were few and far between. Now, however, women make up a significant number of America's forces and are also in harm's way during their military commitment.

MICHIGAN STATE POLICE

GENERAL ORDER

NO. 54

April 25, 1941

Subject: Confirmation of Probationary Troopers,

To: Members of the department.

1.   Effective April 22, 1941, the following Probationary Troopers were confirmed:

Trooper Walter Barkell	Trooper Melvin G. Kaufman
Trooper Willard E. Barrett	Trooper Russell I. Leemgraven
Trooper Robert H. Bilgen	Trooper Kenneth J. Longstreet
Trooper Jasper D. Brouwers	Trooper Raymond E. McConnell
Trooper Orie C. Clark	Trooper Agustine M. McLean
Trooper Daniel J. Comrie	Trooper William L. Mann
Trooper Charles G. Conn	Trooper Donald J. Marion
Trooper William W. Crawford	Trooper Walter A. Moore
Trooper William P. Daugharty	Trooper Andres S. Muth
Trooper Edsel R. Duvall	Trooper Lancelot R. Neff
Trooper Milton D. Eddy	Trooper John M. Nemrava
Trooper David J. Feldkamp	Trooper Russell Olson
Trooper William F. Filter	Trooper Floyd J. Paruch
Trooper William R. France	Trooper John T. Pawielski
Trooper Clifford F. Goodnuff	Trooper Frank J. Sepanik
Trooper Garl G. Gray	Trooper Michael J. Sibal
Trooper Kenneth L. Gray	Trooper Francis E. Simoneau
Trooper Ernest V. Green	Trooper Wallace S. Smyczynski
Trooper Gordon E. Grinwis	Trooper Peter Waisanen
Trooper Frank S. Harris	Trooper Russell T. Weaver
Trooper Urban H. Hebert	Trooper Hans E. Wiebrecht
Trooper Donald E. Hermanson	Trooper Jack D. Wood
Trooper Lloyd M. Huff	Trooper Joseph S. Zimmer

Oscar F Olander

COMMISSIONER.

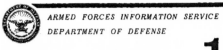

FACT SHEET 1

Help Wanted: MEN

THE POLICE RECRUITING PROGRAM

Secretary of Defense Robert S. McNamara has announced a program in which the Services will assist civilian police agencies in bringing their forces up to strength. Under it, servicemen who receive a firm employment or training offer from a legally constituted City, County, State, or Federal government law enforcement agency can be released up to 90 days earlier than their scheduled separation date.

This program will offer servicemen about to be released from active duty the opportunity to aid their communities in their fight against crime as members of local police forces.

The program is being implemented at the request of President Johnson in an effort to help fill some 15,000 vacancies in police agencies throughout the nation.

Officials of police agencies will be permitted to interview and examine prospective candidates at military installations, but a serviceman can also make direct arrangements with any qualified police agency of his choice. Although the program was initially aimed at strengthening major metropolitan cities' police forces, provisions have been made to include every legally constituted public police agency in the nation. No early release dates will be made to those who desire private police employment.

HOW TO ENTER THE PROGRAM

If you are interested in serving on a particular force such as the one in your hometown, you should either write a letter or send the attached form to the police agency where you are seeking employment, requesting additional employment information.

Figure 1.A

As a part of applying for employment as a police officer you will probably be asked to complete a detailed application form, to take a written examination, to undergo a physical examination, and to participate in a personal interview with police officials.

Your Service is prepared to assist in this processing by providing physical examination facilities and written test facilities as a minimum.

Once you have received a firm offer of employment or notice of training, you should contact your personnel officer who will assist you in your application for early separation. However, you cannot apply more than 180 days before your scheduled date of separation, although you can make inquiries to police departments at any time. Remember, you must make application for early release, and have a firm offer of employment by an authorized police agency. You must also have been counseled concerning fraudulent separation.

TIME OF RELEASE

If you have 90 days or less Service time remaining, you will be released early in the following circumstances:

o You will be released at least 10 days prior to a specific reporting date for employment or training.

o You will be released as soon as administratively feasible if you are offered immediate employment or training.

All applications will be processed through channels to be established by the Services.

WHEN YOU ARE A POLICEMAN

As a member of a police force you will have the satisfaction of serving your community as a member of an honorable and dedicated profession. You will receive a starting pay higher than the average salary of today's workers, together with many fringe benefits such as--annual vacation, sick leave, paid hospitalization benefits for you and your family, a retirement pension program, job protection, uniform allowances, and paid holidays.

The work of a policeman is highly important in our society. It can be an interesting and rewarding career. If you are interested, you must take the first step. Fill out the attached form and send it to the police agency in which you are seeking employment.

Figure 1.B

WHAT IS WRONG WITH LAW ENFORCEMENT TODAY?

The biggest problem with police work today is the fear of civil liability and ATTORNEYS!

Every policy or procedure that a department has is usually derived from some complaint or lawsuit. Of course, I understand and even expect an attorney or citizen to hold an officer accountable for his actions, but cops are AFRAID to take action!

I jokingly told one assistant chief I was dealing with while representing an officer on a misconduct complaint, that we only need one policy statement. That is: "THOU SHALT NOT DO ANYTHING THAT DOES NOT WORK OUT SUCCESSFULLY OR GETS US SUED."

The policy manuals now are so thick that they don't fit in briefcases or even lockers.

I am deeply troubled by the number of officers who are trying to get out of uniform and into a less-harmful position.

I'm not talking about physical harm, but rather out of harm's way when it comes to lawsuits or complaints. While doing research for this book, I spoke with many officers who were planning on making their escape from uniform soon after their probationary period was up. Sure it's okay to have career goals and in some cases look for the better days off to be with your family, but everyone can't be a detective. We have to find a way to keep the experienced troops on the street. I can't blame them for bailing out, because I understand their concerns about being sued.

Years ago, when a wife kissed her officer husband goodbye and sent him off on his shift, she told him she loved him and to be careful. Now the disclaimer includes "DON'T DO ANYTHING TO GET US SUED."

People sitting in judgment of the police usually have not had any personal interaction with an officer. These are people who either volunteered to sit on one of these committees or couldn't figure out how to dodge jury duty.

These people then have to rely on what they have heard about the police from the media, word of mouth, or from the movies. When was the last "cops and robbers" movie that you have seen where the screen writer didn't feel it necessary to have a dirty or evil cop as the villain?

Striking Distance, Speed, The Gauntlet, and *Me Myself and Irene* are all examples of movies with a cop for the bad guy.

By word of mouth, I mean people telling their side of story when talking about how unfairly they were treated by a police officer.

POLITICS AND POLICE WORK

Politics have always played a role in law enforcement. Although our oath and hopefully our characters say that we should treat everyone equally and fairly, it doesn't seem to always work out that way if someone has the ear of a politician.

EXAMPLE:

I was sent a copy of an e-mail where officers were being instructed not to take any enforcement action at a local bookstore where sexual misconduct was suspected. The e-mail said that our department had an agreement with the gay and lesbian community that we would give them a heads-up prior to any inspection. The inspections are required by law. How in the world is this fair if we call and tell them to stop their behavior because we're coming?

In the old days, this would have been known as CORRUPTION!

<u>EXAMPLE:</u>

In another incident, two officers who were known as being tough on drunk drivers — and their records proved it — were swiftly transferred out of an area where several DUI-related incidents and accidents were occurring. I asked one of the officers if he knew why, and he candidly told me that the gay and lesbian bar owners had complained to City Hall that too many gays were being arrested. This area did have a lot of gay bars, but the officers had no way of telling who was gay or straight. Even if they did, does that make drunk driving okay?

I asked the officer if he had a problem if I contacted Mothers Against Drunk Driving and got their view on this, but he asked me not to, so I honored his wishes. He was afraid he would be transferred even deeper into the bowels of the department.

I am not going to name the department here, because I don't want to embarrass or offend the other hardworking officers of the force, but I will keep this information in my credibility safe in case I ever need it.

Often, the police wind up handling anything that someone else either didn't want to do or couldn't afford to do. Just before I retired, the mental health community pushed the passing of a law requiring the police to transport the suspected mentally ill or someone petitioned for mental health evaluation, to a mental health facility. This was also interpreted that the police would have to transport the mentally ill from one facility to another, if it was for mental health treatment.

I often felt that they were being taken from one facility to another simply because their insurance ran out. Nevertheless, what was happening was that we were getting tied up with these "ambulance runs." I can tell you days when there was no one left in my squad area to respond to any other type of calls, emergency or not. About 50,000 people were left without police protection, hoping that a unit from another area could pick up the slack. This also was a crap shoot, because it wasn't often that we weren't all busy with something. Calls could be held for hours if they weren't of an emergency nature.

IMMIGRATION. With immigration becoming a hot button in law enforcement, I am concerned that laws will be passed or interpreted that mandate an officer begin arresting an undocumented person. Working in a border state, we encountered this problem daily. I don't have a political view on this one way or the other, or at least one that I will share in the book. However, keep in mind I just described days where we were all tied up transporting the mentally ill. How in the world could we function efficiently as a police agency if we were then tasked with rounding up thousands of suspected undocumented aliens?

In my early days of looking into becoming a law enforcement officer, I looked into the border patrol, but everyone I knew, including some agents themselves, discouraged me from applying. The agents candidly explained how frustrating their job was. They were arresting the same person over and over again, sometimes several times in the same day. When I speak of recruiting crisis, I think the border patrol will eventually have the same problem. I was listening to a talk show one day; a politician was discussing the problem with patrolling our borders. He recommended that people have to serve a specific number of years, similar to a military draft, as a border patrol agent. How ridiculous is this! A border patrol agent is a law enforcement officer who must pass all kinds of background checks and be dedicated to his profession.

They face danger and temptations daily. What kind of a cop would you get if you drafted them?

The following page is to act as a guide when you review the actions of a police officer. Mark it and refer to it often when reviewing each act or incident in the book. The use-of-force section will have its own checklist. This is to get you thinking out of the box and without preconceived ideas, words, or phrases.

To properly review an officer's action, I want you to get away from some of the standard words and phrases you have previously applied or associated with police work. For example, POLICE BRUTALITY. This is usually thought of as some type of misconduct on the officer's part. Police work is often BRUTAL. If the officer doesn't win the encounter, then he or she is of no good to you!

COMMON WORDS/PHRASES:	CHANGE TO:
Police Brutality	Excessive Force
Shoot To Kill	To Stop The Attack Deadly Force
Blame	Accountable
Civil Disobedience	Riot/Assault, Etc.

(They're committing crimes, not being naughty.)

CONDUCT/MISCONDUCT

This is a simple concept. Conduct is doing something and misconduct is doing something wrong. It's not quite that easy when it is applied to a police investigation. There is a category known as "conduct unbecoming an officer." This can become a catch-all when it comes to a citizen filing a complaint against an officer. I was once told that the definition of conduct unbecoming is "anything the complaining citizen feels it is."

The "customer is always right" theory is a dangerous concept when applied to law enforcement.

After the Rodney King incident and the Christopher Commission that followed, many police agencies reacted by having easier methods for a citizen to bring a complaint or grievance against an officer. That's fine if there is legitimate misconduct, but often the complaints are simply made to harass the officer who called someone down on their behavior.

Below are actual complaints received by police departments.

COMPLAINT:	COMMENTS:
The Officer struck the curb while making a u-turn, I want him checked out in case he is drunk.	
The officer spit her gum out of the window.	
The officer didn't have his hands at the 10/2 position on the steering wheel.	Not illegal for anyone
I'll admit I lied but I didn't like the way the officer asked me if I was lying.	The officer was warned to be cautious about offending folks
I asked the officers to make my son leave the house, but I also asked them to make him take clean socks and underwear and they didn't.	
The officer turned his back on me while I was yelling at him.	
The officer appeared to be angry when he was punched in the face.	I would be too
I demanded to be given a ticket and the officer wouldn't write it.	You can't please some people

DISCIPLINE

Obviously, if an officer violates policy with malice or in bad faith, he needs to be held accountable for his actions. I believe that a police officer should be held to a higher standard of conduct, But police management often holds the officer to an unreasonable standard just to please someone applying pressure, or to give the appearance that we are swiftly dealing with our "bad apples." If an officer is dirty or steals or is brutal for fun, then the system should act quickly. I'll book the offender myself, but in my thirty-four-plus years on the job, I can count on one hand the number of officers I saw go bad.

The discipline being handed out is for minor infractions that would not be an issue in any other business. The example I gave about the officer offending the suspect who lied was not only stupid, but it affects good old-fashioned police work. Calling someone on his lie is necessary if you're going to get at the truth. I represented this officer, who was clearly gun-shy after this incident.

I asked the management involved in this investigation what words the officer should have used to get to the truth. They couldn't agree on those themselves. One suggested that the officer ask if the suspects words were "accurate." ACCURATE? These are street people; they might think accurate is a CAR!

It was early on in his career, and he told me he had learned a valuable lesson: not to create waves. As a citizen, you should expect management to back up the officers if they acted in good faith, or you'll have an ineffective force.

Because of an agency's desire to keep a clean department and reputation with the public, they often go too far. The most ridiculous case of an agency's attempt to assure others that they are policing their own came to me from an officer in my own station who was accused of damaging his own radio. The officer was a rather large man, and as he was leaving the stall in the restroom, he had to turn sideways. In doing so, he damaged the glass faceplate to the radio when he bumped it against the countertop.

When he took the radio into the property room to have it repaired or replaced, he told the rather embarrassing story to the clerks. Everyone had a good laugh, but then later, the suspicious mind of some bean counter kicked in, and they figured he must be lying to cover something up.

So what did the department do? They returned to the scene of the crime and began measuring the width of the stall and, you guessed it, measuring the size of the officer's rear end. I'm pretty sure this isn't what the Christopher Commission had in mind when it comes to holding an officer to a higher standard.

My only formal discipline in my thirty-four-plus years fell into the category of NEGLECT OF DUTY. When I was served notice of this, I thought I must have really screwed up and done something terrible, like not going to someone's aid when they needed help. The reprimand read: "Your locker was found to be unlocked when the Commander went into the locker room; count two, failed to control a city weapon; count three, misuse of city equipment. (The lock, I figured.)

RISK OF LABELS

When a department finds that their officer violated a policy, even one as minor as offending a suspect, it could have long-reaching consequences. In a previous court case, now referred to as the Brady case, the witness's credibility became an issue. The Brady case has expanded to law enforcement and anything that could challenge the officer's ability to testify. The officer's credibility and moral turpitude is offered into evidence or often brought to light in the discovery phase of the process before trial begins. The prosecutor is obligated to notify the defense of any issues the officer in the case might have that could be challenged or used to rebut his testimony.

We all saw in the O.J. Simpson case how the "TRY THE STATE" theory works. One of the detectives in the case had previously made a stupid racial remark. That remark had an effect on the entire case by tainting his testimony and throwing a shadow of doubt on the evidence he had discovered.

There are issues that are not as clear as the Simpson case, which might affect the officer's worth. Having an extramarital affair, making an off-color remark at roll call, or swearing could land the officer on the Brady list under the moral turpitude section. If an officer lands on this list, maintained by the county attorney's office, the officer could conceivably be a non-testifier and of no worth to his agency.

Below is a summary of an actual complaint letter (partial) from a citizen to the mayor of a large city, complaining about the actions, or inactions, of the police. The officer who brought this to me was looking for advice as to whether or not to sue the citizen. When dealing with citizen complaints, the department must look at any policy violations. Simply, the letter writer's opinion is not, or at least should not be, enough to discipline an officer. As far as a police officer filing a lawsuit, the courts look at whether or not the letter was malicious in nature and beyond what a public servant is expected to be subjected to. No court or department wants to restrict the ability of citizens to express their concerns on an officer's behavior.

I advised this officer to grin and bear it, and that hopefully the department will see through motive. See if you can pick out the pieces that I had my concerns with.

A citizen wrote a letter to the Mayor of the city and complained that the officers did not take the proper action, or the action that he, the complainant believed was the appropriate course of action. The complaint involved a neighbor of the complainant driving recklessly in the area and the complainant believed him to be drunk. The complainants wife confronted the neighbor about his conduct and also complained about loud music.

The wifes actions didn't seem to do the trick so the complainant and another neighbor returned and again confronted the neighbor. They then returned home to watch for the police.

Officers responded and arrived just as the neighbor(suspect) had returned home but was out of the car and on his way into the house.

The officers did not witness any driving behavior and most likely could not have taken action for his driving offenses. The officers warned the neighbor about his actions and then arranged for a family member to come and take him to their home because he was somewhat despondent over marital problems.

The officers contacted the complainant and explained their decision on why they allowed a family member to take the person to another location. The complainant suggested that the next time he saw this type of behavior he would "take care of it himself" and went on to tell the officers that he would tear the radio out of the neighbors car. The officers felt it necessary to caution the complainant about those types of threats but it seemed as if everything had calmed down and the officers went on to another call for service.

In his complaint to the Mayor, the neighbor implied that he should have received better treatment because he was white and the offending neighbor was a Spanish speaker and went on to make other racial and cultural comments. He summarized his complaint by suggesting that the officers be suspended for "reverse discrimination and neglect of duty"

Are you beginning to get the idea of what the police face when trying to serve the public? In this case, the officers only witnessed the suspect pull into his own driveway and go into the house. Although a case might be made for being in "actual physical control of a vehicle while intoxicated" it would be a tough one to prove in court.

The officers made a compassionate judgment call, and based on the subject's emotional state, arranged for a family member to come and get him and to look after him. They also suggested domestic counseling.

The loud music complaint is one heard often by police officers across the country. The problem with enforcing this code is that "loud or unreasonable" is an opinion, usually of one neighbor pitted against another. In my thirty-five years on the job, I never saw a conviction for a loud noise complaint.

Now let's look at the issues. In Opinion 1, the wife goes over and confronts the man on his own property. This man already has personal problems and has been drinking; can you see where a confrontation might occur?

Opinion 2 is similar. Now the caller and another male neighbor go over to enforce their own interpretation of a loud noise.

And Opinion 3: The caller lets the officers know that he was going to use force and commit criminal damage to get his way, and can't understand why the officers would even consider arresting him (a white guy) for taking matters into his own hands.

The officers did not witness the loud music, had little to go on with the drunk driving, and were faced with deciding how best to handle the matter for everyone. Having been told the threats by the neighbors to do damage and assault, they are obligated to if not act, at least caution the neighbors from these types of statements.

Remember, a police officer's primary job is to "keep the peace."

This complaint letter is also a good example of a racial profiling issue that we will discuss later. The caller/letter writer believed race was an issue in the officer's decision. I seriously doubt that.

USE OF FORCE (CHECKLIST)
CONTINUUM OF FORCE/RANGE
OF RESPONSE

AUTHOR'S PHILOSOPHY: The use of force is a statutory response to the fight-or-flight syndrome. A police officer doesn't have the luxury to flee, thus using force to affect an arrest or prevent an attack on him or a citizen is mandated, and could be a neglect of duty or nonfeasance issue.

MARK THIS PAGE FOR REVIEWING SCENARIOS.

DON'T THINK THAT YOU MUST ALWAYS START AT THE BEGINNING OR THE BOTTOM OF THE CHART. YOU MIGHT HAVE TO JUMP DIRECTLY TO DEADLY FORCE.

POLICIES AND DEFINITIONS MAY VARY FROM DEPARTMENT TO DEPARTMENT AND STATE TO STATE. CHECK YOUR OWN DEPARTMENT'S POLICIES AND APPLICABLE STATE STATUTES.

CONTINUUM OF FORCE
OFFICER PRESENCE:
Verbal skills

Compliance

Authority

SOFT EMPTY HAND CONTROL:

Restraints

Pressure points

Techniques that have a minimal chance of injury

CHEMICAL AGENTS:

Mace/pepper spray

TASER

HARD EMPTY HAND CONTROL:

Strikes

IMPACT WEAPONS:

Batons

Flashlight

Etc.

STUN BAG:

Non-lethal bullets

K9:

Dog bite

CAROTID CONTROL TECHNIQUE:

Pressure applied to carotid artery

(check policy)

DEADLY FORCE:

Firearm

Other

AGAIN REMEMBER, YOU MAY NOT HAVE THE TIME TO START AT THE BOTTOM, OR IF YOU DID, IT MIGHT NOT HAVE WORKED!

USE OF FORCE

What would you do to survive? What force would you personally use to protect yourself or a loved one? Could you or would you use deadly force?

After 9/11, many people have probably thought about that possibility and even have a plan in mind if they are taking a flight in the near future. Anyone moving too fast toward the front of the plane could face the wrath of dozens of fearful fliers. Even if you urgently need to use the restroom, move slowly toward the front of the plane.

Using force, especially deadly force, can change a police officer's life forever, even if the officer has been cleared by his department and any other reviewing authority. Many officers cannot return to work after taking a life, due to post-traumatic stress.

Applying force to a suspect ALWAYS has the potential of destroying an officer's career.

When it comes to reviewing the use of force, there is a potential of the decision-makers being influenced if the incident is intense and videotaped. I don't like it when an incident is referred to as "caught or captured on tape" This implies the officer did something wrong. Remember, he probably knows he is being taped; it is usually done from his own patrol car.

Consider that he is doing what he believes is necessary to survive.

There was an incident in Ohio where several officers were using batons to contain a combative suspect. It didn't look pretty, but as a police officer reviewing this tape, I could see that ALL of the officers were striking the suspect in areas they were trained to do so and avoiding striking him in the head. They were simply trying to get him into custody.

He later died, but I personally doubt the batons used had anything to do with it.

When I listened to the news account and the Monday morning quarterbacks the following day, one particular commentator upset me with his take on the incident. He said that they shouldn't have beaten this poor guy so badly and they should have "simply shot him once in the foot." He was dead serious on this. This was clearly an incident where the officers were attempting to avoid deadly force.

Later in this chapter, we will discuss how foolish and ineffective the "shoot him in the foot" theory is. Remember now, it's guys like this commentator who could be on a jury or committee that will have control of the officers' career and freedom later.

OFTEN-ASKED QUESTIONS:

Q. WHY DON'T POLICE SHOOT TO WOUND, NOT KILL?

Q. WHY CAN'T THEY SHOOT THE GUN OUT
OF THE SUSPECT'S HAND?

Q. WHY WAS IT NECESSARY TO FIRE SO MANY SHOTS?

Q. COULDN'T THE OFFICER HAVE TRIED
SOMETHING ELSE?

These are all probably legitimate questions for the layman. A police officer is not trained to shoot to kill; he is trained to shoot to stop the assault. We shoot at center mass of the suspect because it lessens the chance of missing and targets more vital organs. Shooting a gun out of someone's hand is TV stuff. It's a small target, and if the officer misses, he could increase the risk to himself and to anyone nearby.

Note: One of the editors from my publishing company asked for clarification on what I meant about officers not being trained to "shoot to kill" and then stating that we target vital organs, which "could kill" This is a legimate question and also shows me that my publishing company is on the ball.

Let me see if I can clear it up a little. Targeting the "center mass" or torso of the suspect makes it more likely that the officers will hit their target and hopefully the force will disable the suspect with one or more shots if necessary.

The officer can then subdue the suspect further with handcuffs or restraints and then work to sustain life and render aid. Once the threat is over the officers are obligated to aid the suspect.

Shooting to kill would be similar to taking a shot at the head. There would be little chance to revive the suspect or sustain life with that shot. I know this is difficult to understand but I have been involved in use of force incidents where the force did disable the suspect and then myself and other officers rendered aid to the suspect. With that being said there may be an occasion where an officer might have to use deadly force and target the suspects head. This could be an incident where the suspect is wearing body armor (something that is being encountered often now by officers) or the fact they simply cannot bring the suspect down any other way.

I reinterate. We are not taught to shoot to kill.

Could the officer have done something else? He probably already tried that and it didn't work, or he had no choice but to go directly to deadly force because of the suspect's actions.

SO MANY SHOTS

Remember, an officer is firing to stop the threat. One or two rounds may not do it. When a suspect decides to fight it out, it is often done when he is chemically altered. There have been stories of suspects withstanding dozens of shots, and I personally know several police officers who have been shot multiple times (four or five hits) and survived. A police officer doesn't have the luxury of being doped up at the time.

TRUE STORY:

One night, when I was working shift three, a call came in of a possible homicide, with a woman and child being shot. The first officer to arrive at the scene was on his first night solo. When he got out of the car, he was confronted by a man pointing something at him and demanding that the officer give up his gun.

The man was standing in what is known by experienced shooters as the "shooter's point shoulder stance." Any shooter or trained police officer would suspect this as a gun attack.

The officer radioed a frantic call for help and then dove for cover. I arrived less than a minute later and yelled at the suspect, who then turned his attention to me. It didn't work as it was supposed to, because this suspect — who we later learned was attempting "suicide by police" — ran toward me.

I dove behind my patrol car and we had a standoff on each side of the car. I was already thinking liability and worse, and didn't take the shot when I had a chance. He continued to pop up on the side of the car, pointing at me, but I didn't react. Later, a brave command officer ran to the side of the car that I was on, so that I was not alone. I told him that I couldn't be sure what the guy had in his hand. The boss told me not to worry about that and to "take the shot the next time." The next time the suspect popped up, pointing at me, I fired. I missed. I struck the roof of my own patrol car that I was hiding behind. This was enough, however, to send the suspect running. He was later tackled and subdued by other officers.

We all survived this, and it was later determined that what he was holding was a pair of child's underwear wrapped around his index finger. He told investigators that he wanted it to look like a gun so we would kill him, and "we screwed it up for him." We also later found out that there was no homicide. He told the 911 operator that to make it more realistic.

The Use of Force Board cleared me of the shooting, but remember, I missed. Had I not missed, I'm sure that public opinion and pressure would have caused me to face harsher review.

I could have written the headlines on that one myself.

POLICE SHOOT TROUBLED UNARMED MAN.

Lots of jokes followed that week, including someone drawing a bull's-eye around the hole in my patrol car roof. I could live with that, though. The suspect's wife wrote a complaint letter to the mayor, complaining that I missed, and suggested I go back to the range to learn how to use my gun better. She also blamed me for any future domestic violence beatings that she might receive.

I can almost guarantee you that if I had struck her husband that night, she would have sued me and the department for loss of income and lack of companionship.

In another incident, I met with an officer soon after he had been involved in an incident where an elderly man had been threatening people with a gun. The officer said that when he arrived, he saw that the suspect was pointing a handgun at another officer. This officer yelled at the suspect, and the suspect turned his attention and his weapon toward this officer. Neither officer fired their weapons.

The suspect eventually gave up without incident and without anyone getting hurt. While I was complimenting the officer, I asked him why he hadn't fired his weapon when he had the chance. He said that he could only think of what he would face later, and said he actually saw headlines: POLICE KILL DISTURBED ELDERLY MAN, ARMED WITH REPLICA GUN.

Yes, in this case, it turned out that the gun the suspect was holding was a non-functional replica, but the officers had no way of telling that night. It was another case of attempted suicide by police. These officers, or at least the one I interviewed for my book research, were willing to risk their own lives to avoid review.

Remember, you are going to be doing some of these scenarios and making decisions that you will only be acting and role-playing with little stress. Your decisions won't cost someone their life!

Law enforcement has always had to deal with the aftermath of a deadly encounter with a suspect, whether it is headlines, civil suits, or in some rare cases, prosecution of the officer. Since the Rodney King incident, police officers face much closer review.

After the Rodney King incident, and the continuous playing of the video on TV, I spoke with a producer from CNN. I predicted that the officers would be tried in a local court, and if a guilty verdict was not reached, there would be riots. I also predicted that there would not be an adequate response from the police department, because their command structure or politicians would fear additional criticism. In the riots and mayhem to follow, the LAPD was criticized for their less-than-aggressive response to the chaos.

As we all watched on national television, a truck driver named Reginald Denny was pulled from the cab of his truck and severely beaten. Any experienced police officer would tell you that the proper response to aid this victim could have been deadly force. Would an L.A. officer be willing to use deadly force at this point, when the riots started over the use of non-lethal force?

I have personally refused to go to L.A. after that incident, because I fear that the cops have been beaten down so badly that they might not react if necessary. I know several fine, dedicated, caring, brave L.A. cops who got an unfair shake from this, but my fear still stands. L.A. is not in my travel plans.

Shortly before finishing this book, one of the most tragic days in the history of my department occurred. Three officers who had responded to a man-with-a-gun call were shot, with two of the young officers dying of their wounds. All three officers were from my station, and I was becoming close to one of them. A fourth officer was seriously injured in a traffic accident as he responded to the scene.

When the three officers arrived at the scene, they found that one victim was already down from gunfire, and information was given to them that the shooter was in a nearby apartment and possibly had another hostage.

A decision was made by these officers to enter immediately without waiting for our special assignments unit, known by many as SWAT. They were immediately met with gunfire.

Their decision to enter is now being questioned, but please remember what I've been saying throughout this book: You have only seconds to decide a course of action that will be reviewed, studied, and used for training later.

Only weeks before this incident, officers were criticized for not entering soon enough during a standoff at a domestic violence incident where someone eventually did die.

INCIDENT:

Just prior to my retiring from the force, I responded to a report of an armed robbery in progress at a central city drugstore. I was first to arrive and was the senior officer at the scene, when we determined that the suspect was still inside and in fact was armed. He was holding at least four employees hostage, with dozens of other shoppers apparently unaware of what was taking place.

I made a decision not to enter, because he apparently knew we were there, by the conversation on the phone with 911. If we entered, we could have forced his hand. He was able to see everything in the store from where he was standing, because of large security mirrors on the back walls. For every action, there is a reaction, and our presence could have caused him to use deadly force.

Every time the front doors opened automatically for a customer to come out, we emotionally readied ourselves for a confrontation. The suspect could put on one of the store vests and try to get out, with us thinking he was just an escaping hostage. All these things have to be factored in when making the decision.

At one point, he fired out the window at us, but no one was hurt. Eventually, he decided it was futile to try to get the money and drugs he had come for, and ended the standoff by taking his own life.

I didn't sleep for two nights after that, thinking about whether I made the right call or not. I could only imagine what the hostages were thinking as to why we weren't coming to their assistance.

Later, I went back to the store and spoke with them with tears in my eyes, and explained my thought process. I told them that we didn't want to force his hand, and that we felt the pharmacist was doing a good job of reasoning with him, and also that we had an entry plan if we heard gunshots; but in reality, that might have been too late. They said they understood, but I'm not sure I would have, if one of my loved ones was in the store.

SHOOTING AT MOVING VEHICLES

One area that draws a lot of criticism is when an officer uses deadly force by firing at a suspect in a moving vehicle.

Even the experts are split on this one. I have strong concerns about shooting at cars. When an officer fires his weapon at a suspect in a vehicle, it must obviously be justified, and he must explain why he felt deadly force was appropriate.

My concerns with shooting at a car are these: What happens to the moving vehicle if you hit the suspect and he no longer has control of the tons of steel moving down the road?

If you miss, could the round deflect and strike another officer or citizen?

When an officer already has his weapon in his hand, following whatever felony has led him to be making this decision, adrenaline alone could cause the officer to respond with deadly force. If other officers are present when a shot is fired, a syndrome known as "contagious fire" could occur. That is where one officer realizes someone is shooting and he also fires.

I have found myself in front of moving vehicles before, and managed to get out of the way. I lived to fight another day. With that being said, it is important that if you find yourself sitting in review of an officer who has fired on a moving vehicle, remember the checklists and ask a few more questions. Was the officer in fear for his life? Would deadly force be reasonable and necessary?

One troubling area for those who represent law enforcement officers is the fact that many cops are afraid to admit that they were AFRAID. We recruit aggressive folks to put on the uniform, so that they don't run from danger. Command presence is pounded into their heads every day in the academy, but not every bad guy gives up or surrenders. If an officer takes the stand during his testimony, please remember that he might not want to admit he was scared. Put yourself in his position; would you have been scared in a similar situation?

Training and experience are not a factor, because we recruit from the human race. Everyone's fears are different.

INCIDENT:

When I was a teenager, I was at a Michigan State Police post, visiting my father, when a motorist came sliding in and said that his wife had been shot. She was the passenger in the front seat. Shortly thereafter, a police car from another agency pulled in and told us that he had fired at a fleeing felon and believed his bullet had deflected into this car. The officer felt terrible, but the motorist seemed to understand. Remember, this was back in the '60s. Understanding isn't so common nowadays.

Later in my early days as a deputy sheriff, I used to love it when fleeing suspects went into that same jurisdiction, because we knew that agency didn't mess around, and they would be shooting out tires or radiators. I strongly believe they saved lives by ending those pursuits quickly.

The shooting-of-tires tactic isn't often used nowadays, mainly because it usually requires two officers in a car, and most departments now are single-man units, and also policies usually prohibit this.

DOES THREATENING TO USE DEADLY FORCE WORK?

When I first entered police work, one officer could hold his own with a crowd. The simple racking of a shotgun could often deter the crowd or a suspect from resisting.

The next time you watch a mob on television, looting a store or assaulting others, watch as the police — almost helpless to stop them — gather only to protect themselves from harm. There is basically no way to stop a rampaging mob, who usually outnumber the police ten times over, until enough officers, or maybe even the military, arrive for a show of force. And even then, it is only to use non-lethal tools to disperse the crowd.

Crowds, and especially those who have done their homework, know that the police will not use deadly force to stop their behavior. I also believe they are also motivated by the fact that they know the courts usually don't hand down stiff sentences for "civil disobedience." Remember, in my checklist, I want you to change civil obedience to the crime they are actually committing — assault, arson, riot, trespass. The police will always be criticized following a use-of-force incident following one of these incidents. Seattle P.D. was criticized once for using too much force and then again for not using enough force and allowing the crimes to occur.

How could they win with that type of logic? It used to be the criticism was just that: someone, not in the know, criticizing a cop's actions, but now it takes on new meanings when the chief of police could be fired for simply not performing the way a politician thinks he should have, or an officer facing charges or discipline for doing what he thought was the right thing during the stress of the moment.

The use of deadly force can affect a police officer for the rest of his career, and he may not be able to return to duty.

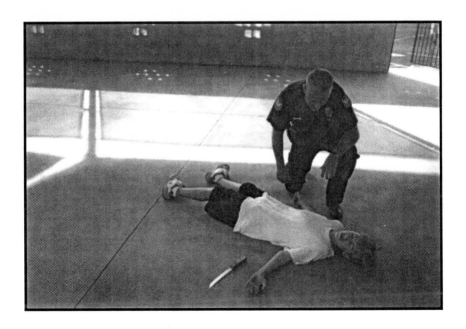

SCENARIOS

Pick someone to be the officer, send two persons out of the room to review (Panel/Jury).

FIRST SCENARIO

You are driving past a school when you see a young man walking toward the front door, carrying what appears to be a rifle. You immediately stop your patrol car and yell commands to the man, ordering him to halt.

You identify yourself as a police officer, even though you are in full police uniform and driving a marked police car. The man keeps walking toward the school, not responding to your commands.

When the subject gets within about ten feet of the door, and just before entering the school, you must decide whether to use deadly force, your only apparent option.

Using deadly force on this subject walking away from you will require you to shoot the subject in the back.

WHAT ACTION WILL YOU TAKE?

(Results are on the following page. Don't cheat.
Work the scenario through and then read the answers.)

SECOND SCENARIO

You respond to a call of an armed robbery in progress at a liquor store. When you arrive, you see a man running from the store and see another man chasing him. The person chasing the other man has a gun in his hand. You identify yourself as a police officer, but the man keeps chasing the other man. He then fires a shot at the fleeing man.

WHAT ACTION DO YOU TAKE?

DO YOU FIRE YOUR WEAPON?

AT WHOM?

Remember, this also most likely will require shooting someone in the back.

SCENARIO RESULTS

I'm going to give you two results. Apply them and then discuss them in your groups. Neither may be right or wrong. You will just have to make a finding/decision.

SCENARIO 1

OUTCOME I

The officer fired his weapon, striking the young man in the back, killing him instantly. The investigation reveals that the young man was seventeen years of age and on his way to play rehearsal with a non-working prop gun. He was also deaf.

Your decisions:

A. Criminal charges

B. Discipline

C. Civil awards

OUTCOME II

The officer chose not to fire his weapon, being uncertain as to what was occurring. The subject entered the school, and within seconds, screams could be heard coming from inside the school. Later, it was determined that the young man was upset with classmates, and brought one of his father's guns to school. Five teenaged students were killed and several others were wounded. The officer's inactions were challenged.

Your decisions:

A. Criminal charges

B. Discipline

C. Civil awards

SCENARIO 2

OUTCOME I

The officer believed that the person being chased was in danger, and fired at the subject with the gun. It turned out that the person with the gun was the store clerk, chasing the robbery suspect. He was only wounded by the officer, but received a severe injury to his leg and may lose the use of it.

Your decisions:

A. Criminal charges

B. Discipline

C. Civil awards

OUTCOME II

The officer was not sure as to who the bad guy was and who the victim was. Within seconds, the suspect with the gun fired, killing the other man who was fleeing. The investigation revealed that the man fleeing was the liquor store owner. He died of his wounds. The suspect was caught later by other officers.

Your decisions:

A. Criminal charges (neglect of duty)

B. Discipline

C. Civil awards

SCENARIO 3

You are called to a residence where a sixteen-year-old boy is threatening suicide. He is armed with a knife, and at the time of your arrival, is threatening no one else. He tells you that he wants you to kill him and that he will attack you if it is necessary to get you to shoot him.

You have these options:

A. Try to talk him out of it and hope that you can avoid using deadly force. Your appearance alone might cause the incident to escalate.

B. Pull back and wait outside the house, hoping that he will calm down.

OUTCOME I

The officer remained inside and tried to convince the young man to drop the knife and seek mental health help. The young man did not respond, and advanced on the officer. The officer retreated as far as he could, but was forced to fire, killing the youth.

Your decisions:

A. Criminal charges

B. Discipline

C. Civil awards

OUTCOME II

The officer decided to try backing out and waiting for other assistance, including mental health specialists. Only seconds later, the young man self-inflicted a knife wound, taking his own life.

Your decisions:

A. Criminal charges

B. Discipline

C. Civil awards

LIABILITY CONCERNS:

I am constantly talking about officers being more concerned about liability issues when making a decision on whether to take actions. In 2004-2005, H.R.218 passed the Senate and became law, allowing for police officers, active and retired, to carry a firearm anywhere in the country, regardless of where they were or had been a sworn officer.

The sponsors of this bill used not only the fact that officers had to concern themselves with threats on their lives from someone they encountered during their career, but also pitched the homeland security benefit of another armed, trained person who might be able to thwart an attack on America.

This is great and understandable logic, but most of the retirees I know do not carry a gun, even in their own jurisdiction where they retired. The fact is that liability has once again affected this well-meaning legislation. If an officer or retired officer believes he is doing the right thing by going to someone's aid, who is going to be there to support him when the lawsuit is filed? The deep-pockets theory for lawyers no longer applies for retirees, so they will have to go after the individual. I didn't trust my agency to stand behind me when I was on the job, let alone now. I pray that my training and desire to help mankind will override my fears of losing everything I own, but I'm not sure. I have set a standard for myself that I will only go to the assistance of someone I personally know, or a loved one. This is a terrible thing to have to admit to, but it is the way that many retired and active officers feel.

I was sitting with a group of officers and retirees one evening at a retirement party, when someone made a joke about the surprise that a bad guy would get if he tried to rob a bar with a room full of armed cops. The laugh turned to disbelief when it was learned that there was not a gun among the ten of us. A sad testimonial to the times.

DRIVING/PURSUITS

I sometimes think that it is easier for a police officer to decide whether or not to use deadly force than it is to have to decide whether or not to chase a fleeing suspect in a vehicle. The what-ifs and unknowns are greater. Every citizen wants an officer to get there quickly when they need help, but quickly turns to thoughts of lawsuit if the officer injures someone in a traffic accident. Police departments across the county face lawsuits over pursuits, even if the suspect is the one who causes the accident.

ACTUAL HEADLINES

OFFICER BLAMED IN MOTORIST DEATH

DEPUTY SHERIFF FOUND GUILTY IN MOTORIST'S DEATH

HIGHWAY PATROLMAN SENTENCED
TO PRISON FOLLOWING DEATH OF MOTORIST

More police officers are killed in motor vehicle accidents than any other line-of-duty incident. Officers, by nature, are aggressive people and want to catch bad guys, or to get there in time to make a difference for someone in need.

Senior officers and training officers must constantly remind the younger troopers to calm down, slow down, and to manage their adrenaline when behind the wheel of a car. The more the siren sounds, the harder the gas pedal is depressed. When you get to the driving scenarios, you will see that it isn't as easy as it appears when deciding to chase or not to chase a fleeing suspect.   .

Why is this person fleeing?

EXAMPLE 1

During a string of takeover armed robberies of banks and credit unions (jump-the-counter), the getaway driver was briefed by the rest of the gang to drive recklessly if the cops came. The gang had done its homework and found that the policy for the police department was to terminate a pursuit if the driving got too dangerous. Unfortunately for the suspects, they encountered an aggressive supervisor, who allowed the pursuit to continue, and they were all eventually caught.

They did, however, cause one serious traffic accident, injuring an elderly woman. During the interview with the suspects, one actually had the nerve to attempt to file a complaint against the officers for catching him. He said the officers violated policy, and the arrests should be invalid. This group was responsible for over a dozen of this type of robbery.

EXAMPLE 2

A thirteen-year-old experienced car thief crashed during a flight from a patrol car and was seriously injured. The young thief demanded to see a supervisor. He complained that the officers were not supposed to chase him for a non-violent felony; again, someone who knew policy. What he didn't know is that he was chased by the highway patrol, which did not have as restrictive policies as the city agency.

EXAMPLE 3

A police supervisor terminated the pursuit of a suspected drunk driver who was driving at twenty miles per hour in a thirty-five zone. This is fifteen miles per hour below the speed limit. Geez, I was fifty-five years old at the time of this one, and I could have parked my car, run alongside of the suspect, and negotiated his surrender.

I understood the young supervisor's thought process, though, because if something goes wrong during one of these incidents, it is the on-scene supervisor who has to answer to the brass.

The true examples that I have given you clearly show that the suspects often know policy and count on the police to back off. Imagine being a kidnapping victim, bound and gagged in the back seat of a car, when it appears as if the police are going to rescue you but the suspects speed away and the officers don't know you were in there. What are your survival chances now?

Some police agencies actually have "no pursuit" policies in place. I don't have enough information or feedback to know how this works, but I can't help but think that their crime rate and vehicle death rate is high.

I had over thirty-four years on the job, and I had to continuously tell myself to slow down while driving to an emergency. The agency I worked for had a fifteen-mph-over-the-speed-limit policy for responding to emergency calls. This includes child drowning, rapes, domestic violence, or child abductions. I contend that a pizza delivery driver goes faster than that to get your pizza to you hot and fresh.

Shortly after retiring, I was headed downtown when I saw a pickup truck approaching in my rear view mirror at a high rate of speed. The truck swung out and passed me on the left in a left-turn-only lane. I was getting ready to "flip him off" — a tactic that I knew better and would have surely been disciplined for if I was still on the force, but I was a civilian now, and I was thinking I'd make up for lost time. My better judgment took over, and I managed to hold my temper. The truck made a quick left turn onto a side street, and then I noticed about a dozen patrol cars and motorcycle units following.

It became clear that this was a fleeing suspect. The department's policy was that pursuits were to be terminated if the fleeing suspect was a "non-violent" suspect. I later learned that this suspect had stolen the truck and was under the influence of meth, a dangerous drug.

In keeping with policy, the officers who had been chasing him went into a "watch only" mode and made no effort to stop his driving. Remember that he was also suspected of being under the influence of drugs, which was clearly a hazardous situation for the rest of the drivers using the roadways, but because of liability concerns, the monitoring supervisors from the original chase ordered the officers to "back off."

The road which he had turned down was a dead-end street and would have been a perfect place to end the flight of this dangerous driver, but none of the more than a dozen officers were willing to risk it and face severe discipline.

The suspect came back out onto a busy city street and continued his erratic driving for almost two hours until he decided to crash through a security gate at one of the nation's busiest airports. After crashing through the gate, he entered an active runway and drove alongside a departing aircraft, now obviously a very dangerous situation.

A brave detective, in an unmarked car, decided it was time to end this flight, and rammed the truck, bringing the chase to a halt. Ramming is strictly forbidden in this department's policy, and shifts all blame and liability to the officer himself. Later, the police department revised their pursuit policy to allow for "ramming" if the suspect enters airport property.

Now go back to the beginning of this chase, where I saw the suspect pull onto a dead-end street. If the officers would have been confident that the agency would have stood behind them, they might have ended this incident before the close call on the runway, besides the hundreds of innocent motorists who were endangered by his driving.

I truly believe that there will have to be more civil suits filed for neglect of duty, for NOT pursuing a fleeing suspect, to turn this permissive type of police work around. I'm almost certain that if the suspect would have played a part in crashing an airplane, the survivors would want someone held accountable. When I gave these next scenarios to a civic group, it got emotional to the point that folks were crying. Let's see how you do with them.

SCENARIO ONE

You are on routine patrol when you see a vehicle parked in a wooded area, well off the beaten path. When you pull up to check out the vehicle, you use your computer to check on the license and find that it is not reported as stolen. As you get out and approach the vehicle, it quickly speeds off, leading you on a pursuit which eventually winds up in a heavily populated area of town. The speeds are becoming dangerous, and the driver of the fleeing vehicle shuts off his lights and begins running stop signs.

Should you continue to chase this vehicle for traffic offenses only?

SEND TWO PEOPLE OUT OF THE ROOM NOW BEFORE THE ACTOR OFFICER DECIDES WHETHER TO CONTINUE THE PURSUIT.

SCENARIO TWO

You are on routine patrol when you see a vehicle traveling at a high rate of speed (approximately sixty-five in a thirty-five zone). The vehicle is weaving and jerking across the center line and all other traffic lanes. You suspect the driver is drunk.

DO YOU CONTINUE THE PURSUIT?

SCENARIO RESULTS

SCENARIO ONE

OUTCOME I

The officers decided that the chase was becoming too dangerous, and in keeping with department policy for "traffic-only" offenses, the officers terminated the pursuit. Within minutes of letting the vehicle go, a broadcast was put out of the exact same description of vehicle. It had just been involved in a child abduction of a four-year-old girl. This was a stranger abduction.

Your decisions:

A. Criminal charges

B. Discipline

C. Civil awards

OUTCOME II

The officers continued the pursuit and the suspect entered an intersection at a high rate of speed, colliding with a family of four. Two persons died in the victim's vehicle.

Your decisions:

A. Criminal charges

B. Discipline

C. Civil awards

SCENARIO TWO

OUTCOME I

The officers determined the driving was too dangerous and terminated the chase. An aircraft was available but could only observe the driving behavior. The suspect went on and struck a pedestrian crossing the street lawfully.

Your decisions:

A. Criminal charges

B. Discipline

C. Civil awards

OUTCOME II

The officers felt they must apprehend this suspect, who was obviously drunk, before he hurt someone. As they reached speeds of over 100 miles per hour, the driver of the patrol car lost control and rolled the cruiser. The driver of the patrol car was seriously injured and the passenger officer was critically injured. The passenger officer is expected to be crippled for the rest of his life.

Your decisions:

A. Criminal charges

B. Discipline

C. Civil awards (passenger officer/family)

NEGLECT OF DUTY

It's not just his actions an officer has to justify; sometimes it's his inactions where he finds himself being reviewed. If an officer decided against taking a specific action because he felt it was unlawful or improper, he might still have to face the music if the caller was right and some crime did occur.

Later, in the racial profile section of this book, I will discuss calls that officers responded to and were faced with contacts that might be looked upon as racial profiling. The officer is subject to any prejudices that the caller might have.

Although there may have been a crime occurring, the officer must weigh reasonable suspicion or probable cause when determining what action to take, or if an arrest is warranted. An anonymous call from a citizen might not be enough for the officer to act.

EXAMPLE

A citizen reports hearing gunshots coming from the back yard of a house. The caller knows that only one guy lives there, so "it must be him." That mentality is not law, and probably won't fly with the prosecutor's office to file charges.

If an officer does manage to make an arrest, it still isn't as easy as just getting the case before a judge or jury. The case has to be reviewed by a prosecutor, or in some cases, the district attorney's office. This is a topic that frustrates many a police officer, because what they believe to be a slam dunk case is often not "filed."

Phrases such as "lacks jury appeal" or "no reasonable likelihood of conviction" are used by prosecutors to turn the case down and not proceed with it to court.

I understand the fact that the prosecutor has to take into consideration time and costs, but I believe we should let the jury decide many of these cases, instead of dumping them before trial. Some of the street thugs I used to deal with actually adopted the term "scratched," which means the prosecutor didn't file. They use that term to either brag or explain why they are free and out of jail.

EXAMPLES OF TURN-DOWNS

Officers arrest four underage boys with four cans of beer. The turn-down reads: No way to determine which boy had which can.

Officers arrest a subject assaulting a doctor during an examination following the suspects arrest on another matter.

The turn-down reads: Although the subject admits he knew he was assaulting a doctor, the jury pool is made up of people who watch TV, and the good doctors on *ER* don't call the police when they are struck.

During a liquor enforcement of an after-hours bar, officers cited the bartender for after-hours sales.

The turn-down reads: No indication in the report as to the distance between the bartender and the customer seated at the bar. [Folks, this should not be a concern; the law says that no one can be in the bar after hours, PERIOD.]

Officers arrest a man in a domestic violence incident where the man (husband) stood outside and banged on the door of an apartment where his wife had gone to hide. He yelled that he was going to kill her if he got in. Police arrived shortly thereafter. He was charged with disorderly conduct, among other charges.

The turn-down read: Did anyone ask him to be quiet?

Why in the world is this important? Even if there was some magic way to calm this guy because a neighbor yelled at him, he was still committing DOMESTIC VIOLENCE, which is a mandated arrest now in most jurisdictions.

People who complain about the police not taking action, or that the subject is out of jail, usually aren't privy to the fact that the officers might have done their job, but it was dumped at another level.

With that being said, I still encourage EVERY police officer to do the right thing, and if an arrest is warranted, take the action. Refer them to the correct authority if it isn't sent up the chain.

EXAMPLE

"The officer didn't do anything when a car made an illegal turn."

I was at the desk when this call came in, so we researched the information because the caller had the car number on the side of the unit. We found that the officers were responding to emergency traffic of a fight in progress, and I tried to explain that to the caller. The caller said he didn't care, that if we continued to overlook violations, they will continue. I suspect that if this caller was waiting at the other end of the line for the officers to respond, he wouldn't understand if they stopped to write a civil infraction ticket.

Personally, I often didn't attempt to stop a red-light runner or other offenses, if the enforcement action might be more hazardous than the offense. Running the light yourself, even if doing so with lights and sirens, you could cause a major accident.

If you wind up sitting in review on a neglect-of-duty "beef," please try to factor in everything the officer knew or didn't know, and if the caller had an axe to grind.

A. Did the officer see the offense?
B. Was there probable cause/reasonable suspicion?
C. Did the officer make the arrest but it wasn't filed?
D. Could the officer take action without the caller's help?
E. Was it illegal (actually a crime)?

If it was pure laziness on the officer's part, then go ahead and hammer him!

When someone is judging an officer on his actions or inactions, it is usually done following some emotionally charged situation. In a recent California case, two officers had stopped a suspicious subject, and they released him because they had nothing to lawfully hold him on. Gut feelings, even if the officers are tenured, are not enough to detain someone.

The subject was later found to have abducted and killed a young girl. The officers had no way of knowing what this person had done. Public outcry demanded that these officers be fired for not preventing the girl's death.

Even today, as I watched the news, I saw the parents of a missing teenager being interviewed. They were criticizing the police for not "making the suspects talk." They related the interview to questioning of a terrorist, and believed someone could force them to confess. I totally feel for these people and understand their frustrations, but it is not the same. If the rubber hose were to be used, the officers would be prosecuted, and any admissions made would be suppressed.

Even the terrorist interview suggestion is not valid. Look at what our military is going through from their critics about detaining and questioning terrorists.

WHERE'S A COP WHEN YOU NEED ONE?

I recently read a story or joke on the Internet about a man who called the police to report a prowler in his garage, and was told by the police that there was no one available to send. The story goes that the man called right back and reported he just shot the man, and several officers then arrived.

What one is supposed to get from the story is that the man was either lied to, that the officers were simply having a cup of coffee and a donut, or that he just wasn't taken seriously.

My explanation is simple. Calls for service are prioritized by the seriousness of the incident. Although having a prowler in one's garage could be serious, it may not be the most serious incident occurring at the time.

Police service is similar to the business community. It is a supply-and-demand issue. Police departments across the country face manpower shortages and budget cuts, so they are forced to deal with less supply than demand.

In the case described on the Internet (if it is true), officers most likely had to break off something else to come to a now-upgraded incident. In other words, someone else had to be dropped down a rung on the priority list because our impatient caller lied to get better service.

Some agencies have gone to limiting the service that they provide, and take many reports by phone. My agency had a unit known as "callback" which took calls such as thefts (without suspects present) and if someone's car was stolen.

Whatever the reason you do not get quick response from the police, I doubt that it is because they simply aren't interested or that they are sitting somewhere having a cup of coffee. Many a donut shop has folded over the fact the cops no longer have time to sit and have a cup and a snack (tongue in cheek)

In the case of the prowler in the garage, most cops would love to handle this call, just for the adrenaline rush of catching an "in-progress crime." Much of police work is after-the-fact report-taking. I used to refer to myself as a CART. That's a computerized, armed report-taker.

The bottom line is: don't lie to get better service. You may very well find yourself on the way to jail for making a false police report. You endanger the officer who will most likely respond in emergency mode, and also might put someone else in harm's way, such as taking an officer away from a domestic dispute that could later turn ugly if the cop leaves.

SCENARIOS

We are going to take this area a little differently. Break up into two groups and tackle these incidents. Assign one group to defend the officer's actions, and the other group will be blaming the officers for the results of the incident. List all of your arguments and then spend ten to fifteen minutes presenting your cases. There may not be a right or wrong answer to these, just opinions and judging of facts.

SCENARIO ONE

Two officers are patrolling a county road and observed a vehicle pulled off into a secluded area. They approach the driver, who is seated alone in the car, and ask him for his license and other papers, which he readily complies with. The license checks out and he has no active warrants. The officers ask him what he is doing, and he says he was just resting from driving a long ways. Still suspicious, one of the officers asks him for permission to search the vehicle. Again, the polite driver says he apologizes for sounding uncooperative, but tells them he knows his rights, and that he does not have to allow a search.

The two deputies discuss their options and decide they do not have enough to force the issue. They leave.

The next morning, the same car is found abandoned in the woods. When investigators opened the trunk, they found a young coed dead inside. The autopsy indicates she was only dead for a few hours, and had most likely been alive when the deputies spoke with the suspect. The suspect was later found to be a recently released sexual predator from another state. Out-of-state records are not available on most police in-car computers.

WHAT ARE YOUR ARGUMENTS FOR AND AGAINST THEIR ACTIONS?

SCENARIO TWO

An officer was dispatched to check welfare on a man who hadn't shown up for work for two days. The caller, who is the man's employer, said that the man lives alone and this is not like him. The employment records indicate he also has no next of kin listed. The responding officer goes to the house and gets no response at the door. He checks all the doors and windows and finds them all to be locked. The officer checks with a couple of neighbors who say that the man keeps to himself usually, and that to their knowledge, no one has a key.

The officer checks with his supervisor and it is decided that they do not have enough information to force entry, which could cause the city to have to pay for damages. They leave.

Several days later, in the summer heat, neighbors report a strong odor coming from the same house. This time, entry is forced, and the man's body is found. It is speculated that the man was alive but unable to move when the first officer responded.

REMAIN IN TWO GROUPS AND ARGUE BOTH DECISIONS WHETHER TO FORCE ENTRY OR WHETHER THE OFFICER ACTED PROPERLY.

DOMESTIC VIOLENCE:

Probably one of the areas most criticized for not taking action is that of domestic violence. Domestic violence is a serious problem and one of the leading causes of death or injury to women. Law enforcement personnel are also often injured on these calls.

Looking back at it now, during my thirty-four years on the job, I can see that we might have had a cynical attitude toward these types of calls, because we couldn't understand why a victim — not always the woman — would stay in an abusive situation. Understanding the cycle of violence helps to understand this, however.

Most police officers would still take actions if they were warranted, but an arrest wasn't always possible. Keep in mind that until the passing of various state laws mandating arrests for domestic violence, officers could only arrest if the crime was committed in their presence. If not, they would have to submit a report to the D.A. or prosecutor for review.

My first arrest following the passage of our state's mandated D.V. law was an obvious assault on a woman by her husband. I was ready for this, and I placed him under arrest. As we were leading him to the patrol car in handcuffs, the wife kept yelling and demanding that we release him. Shortly after yelling "Don't take him," she grabbed me around the neck and rode me halfway to the car.

After getting control of the situation, I opted not to arrest her, because I was pretty experienced by now and I could sense she was acting. She probably felt that System would let her down and she would have to face her husband's wrath when he got out. It is important for an officer to instill in the suspect that the officer or the state is making the mandated arrest, and that the victim/wife could not drop charges if he or she wanted to. Hopefully, this can minimize retaliation later.

There are some serious problems, however, with this mandatory arrest theory. I was sitting in a restaurant one night, in uniform, working off duty, when I was approached by a young man who asked if he could speak with me. He began his conversation by telling me that he "hated my new domestic violence law." I asked him why, and he told me that he could always tell when his mother wanted to be alone for the weekend. She would go into the bathroom, slap herself in the face, bite her lip, and call the cops. He said that we would take his father to jail without listening to reason.

I often wondered how many innocent people got booked because the officers were afraid to call someone on suspicious appearances.

An officer has little recourse other than arrest if a D.V. does occur, even if it is as minor as a food fight. Criminal damage, disorderly conduct, and other offenses besides assault are mandated categories. I used to pride myself on calming folks down during arguments, and even have gone as far as making a pot of coffee in their kitchen to talk through issues. Now, an officer doesn't want to risk it not working out and be charged with neglect of duty if it goes bad later.

Although the legislatures that passed these mandatory laws want you to believe they have fixed a big problem, it is not true. In many cases, if the victim doesn't show up to court to testify, the case is dismissed. In all of my years doing this job and arresting lots of abusive husbands, I have only been to one D.V. trial, and in that case, the victim wife lied. Hearsay rules and the right to confront your accusers still apply to these types of cases.

It is important, however, that you as a police officer do the right thing, and if an arrest is warranted, then make it. Do not worry about the outcome in court; just do what is mandated and expected of you.

NEGLECT OF DUTY REVIEW

MALFEASANCE/NONFEASANCE/ NEGLIGENCE

1. Was it legal?

2. Did the officer have a duty to act?

3. Was it reasonable?

4. Was it within policy?

5. If not within policy, can the officer justify going outside of the guidelines?

6. Was it the right thing to do?

RACE/GENDER/LIFESTYLE PROFILING

There is no other area of concern in law enforcement more sensitive than this one. Law enforcement may never recover from the damage done by the Rodney King incident in Los Angeles. The "post-Rodney King" era police officer is aware that he will be scrutinized and reviewed to a greater degree if a person of color is involved. Lifestyles are also now the subject of some complaints.

What reviewing citizens must keep in mind are the motives for an officer to abuse his or her authority. Most officers know that they might be videotaped or watched by citizens or critics. Would they actually risk losing everything, including their careers or freedom, to treat someone differently based on any personal biases or beliefs?

INCIDENT:

I was listening to a local talk show one morning and the topic of police abuses of minorities was on. I listened to one caller telling the host about an incident where he and another limo driver were racing back to their office when the police appeared. The caller, who was white, said that the officer passed him up and stopped the other driver, who was black. This caller then had to assume that the officer was a racist and targeting the black driver.

It just so happened that I was the officer on this incident. I passed up the first limo to get at the lead one that was driving faster and more erratically. There was no way that I could tell the race of either driver, due to the darkness of night, the heavy tint on the limos' windows, and the speeds they were doing. When I caught up to and contacted the black driver, I chose to just "chew butt" and not cite him, because I often feel I can correct a problem with talk and not ink. I also didn't feel it fair, because I never got the other driver.

I was unable to get through to the talk show to correct this attitude, so many more people were left believing cops stop for race.

When reviewing the complaints about "I was stopped because I am _____," try to remember the checklists (why), then review how the officer handled the incident after the face-to-face.

INCIDENT:

One evening, another officer and I were working off duty (moonlighting), and on the way to a fast-food restaurant where we were hired for security, when we saw a black male running down the railroad tracks, carrying a large box on his shoulder. It was about one o'clock in the morning, so we doubted that this had been a legitimate purchase. When we passed him, we could see that the box was a microwave oven, and assumed he had just visited a boxcar. Both of us had more than thirty years on the job, and it was apparent that we were witnessing a felony. This should have been a simple fix for a couple of dedicated officers, but it didn't work out that way. We began acting like defense attorneys and reviewing our options. We asked each other what would happen if we were wrong. Would he have a complaint? What would happen if he fought and someone got hurt? Would we be covered by insurance? What if he uses the race defense? Would we be in trouble?

By the time we got done with the "what-ifs," he was long gone with his new microwave. We drove on to our job site, laughing so hard, we almost couldn't breathe. I think we both felt we let someone down, but we didn't want to risk being wrong. By the way, I forgot to mention that the other officer with me was black.

INCIDENT:

One morning, as I sat through the questioning of a jury panel for a drunk driving case, I was amazed to hear the defense attorney object to the makeup of the jury. He protested because there were no blacks on the jury. This puzzled me, because the defendant was a fifty-plus-year-old white guy, so during the break, I asked him what the deal was. He told me that it was nothing personal, but that he had a better chance of an acquittal if there was a black person on the panel, because they wouldn't like me because of my color, "blue."

INCIDENT:

I was representing an officer in front of a use-of-force board, following an accidental discharge of his firearm during a fight (no injuries). In my department, all incidents involving discharging of a weapon go before at least one board, and sometimes others. As we entered the room, I noticed the black member of the board give the officer, who was black, a thumbs-up, indicating there was nothing to worry about. With a wink and a nod, it was clear that this was a potential win, even before evidence was offered.

I was happy for the officer, but also could not help but think we were facing a double standard with this type of find.

INCIDENT:

It isn't just persons of color who are complaining, but also lifestyles are becoming a "stopped me because I'm_____
_____" defense. During a defense interview, I was asked if I had seen any bumper stickers or signs on the defendant's car. Since I had already heard of this tactic, I knew where the defense attorney was going with this. It is the "gay defense." I reminded the attorney that his client was doing ninety miles per hour in a thirty-five zone. I was having trouble enough seeing taillights, let alone rainbow stickers. I then reminded the attorney that I gave his client a ride to a friend's home after processing the DUI charge, instead of booking him. That was now tough to defend, because of the face-to-face after the stop.

The area I worked in 2003 was predominantly Spanish. If I did not make an arrest or issue a citation, it often was because the subject was a Spanish speaker, and I couldn't communicate enough to get the job done. This also became a racial challenge as a defense many times. The truth is that these offenders were more likely to catch a break because of the language barriers. Officers would blow off the ticket if they couldn't communicate with the offender, who simply said "no speak English."

Our local highway patrol had a racial profiling form that they have to fill out that is longer than the citation.

If bias or prejudice is a factor in police work, it is more likely because of the attitude of the caller, not the officer. The officer is in a no-win situation when responding to a call that might be based solely on the feelings of the person making the call.

These are actual calls.

A. Black male standing on the corner doesn't look like he belongs in the neighborhood.

B. Black female dressed like a "hooker" walking up and down the street; caller demands she move along.

C. Hispanic male sitting at a bus stop looks like he has a gun under his shirt.

D. Two Hispanic males sitting in a car by caller's house; wants them checked out and made to move.

E. Young black male driving a late-model car doesn't look like he "fits."

Experienced officers and hopefully even the younger ones wouldn't make a stop on the call about the black male not looking like he fits in a certain type of vehicle, but the others are not so easy. What if the callers were right and something happened in their neighborhood? Could the officers now face neglect-of-duty beefs?

When I first became a police officer in 1968, I was fresh out of Viet Nam. There wasn't much training other than: here's your gun and statute book, "go get 'em." I did learn from the old-timers, though, that most of the crimes were being committed by people with long hair. Those hippies and beatniks needed to be watched. I guess even as a young cop, I didn't buy into that, but I didn't want to go against the trend.

Most police agencies have checks and balances in place to make sure that an officer isn't singling out someone based on race, and track the officers' daily contacts. I can tell you honestly that I have backed away from contacts because of fear of complaint.

Before the 9/11 attacks, there wouldn't be an officer I know who would have stopped the hijackers based solely on their appearance. Prior to 9/11, anyone could have boarded an aircraft with a case of box cutters with an advertising slogan on them and have been just fine. During the blame period, we now believe that these guys should have been profiled.

One summer, when I was driving across county in a rented van, I was pulled over in a Southern state by a state trooper. I know I hadn't violated any laws, so I asked the trooper what I had done. I'll admit I badged him at this point. Once he knew that he could talk honestly with me, he told me they had a big drug problem going through their state, and asked me if we had a drug problem in my area. We had a big laugh when I showed him my card that I was assigned to a neighborhood narcotics squad.

The fact is that my vehicle, not me, was profiled because of rented vehicles being used to traffic drugs. I'm not sure I agree with that theory, but I do believe any type of profiling based on race has no place in law enforcement.

RACE/PROFILING REVIEW QUESTIONS

A. What would be the officer's motive?

B. Was the suspect they were looking for a particular race?

C. Could the officer tell the race (time of day/tinted windows)?

D. Does the officer have a complaint history?

E. What is the environment (makeup of area)?

F. What would you do if faced with similar facts?

UNIONS/ASSOCIATIONS/OFFICERS' RIGHTS

When I was a rookie officer, I couldn't see the need for a police union. Why would an officer need union protection if he kept his nose clean and always did the right thing? An association would be all right, because they work toward better salary and benefits, but legal protection isn't necessary if you don't screw up.

I now see where I was way off base. I became a union representative to defend officers from ridiculous, baseless complaints and investigations. Doing the right thing wasn't as clear as I first thought it was going to be. What I thought was the right thing to do, and was common-sense police work, was interpreted differently by citizens and politicians and those within my own department with bars, stars, or stripes. It often becomes easier to just discipline an officer than to fight someone with political clout, even if the officer did nothing wrong.

A police officer must know that if he gets into a jam, there will be someone there with money and resources to defend him. If an officer feels he is not going to be backed or supported and is on his own, human nature might kick in. It is human nature to take the path of least resistance.

You as a citizen can't afford to have an officer weighing all of the potential harm to his career before he makes a decision. Your safety is at risk. I'm not advocating defending an officer against clear misconduct or blatant abuses, but it is important that an officer knows where to turn if he's in a jam. When I was in training to become a union representative, my mentor told me, "It is not your job to get them off from a complaint, it is your job to get them FAIR." I tried to live by that rule on each case I took.

There is a danger, though, with unions becoming too strong and powerful. They can sometimes take on a life of their own. Often, these large police unions become so involved in politics and endorsing political candidates that they forget the everyday business of protecting officers' rights.

The association that I represented was the largest police organization in the state; however, it was my opinion that they were weak at best. Many an officer lost his job to what I believe were poorly investigated complaints or on "he said/she said" allegations. The department often just threw the baby out with the bathwater, instead of trying to show that the officer's action was not misconduct. The mindset of the association was to have a working relationship with the police department. That is an acceptable theory, if both sides played by the rules.

I never saw my association take the department or the city to court when they clearly violated the officer's civil rights or terminated him based on a flawed investigation.

Shortly after leaving the agency, I was contacted concerning a probationary officer who was fired because her immediate supervisor believed she had not been truthful with her during an administrative investigation. The officer and her representative asked for a polygraph examination (lie detector), but the department declined. The officer was fired simply because her immediate supervisor decided she was not being truthful. With our agency, there was no second or independent review. The investigating supervisor was the person who determined guilt. Can you see where this could be a problem?

Why would the supervisor make the allegation, investigate it herself, and then determine that they were wrong from the beginning and exonerate the officer? There are some appeals rights but the track record for our agency and the union were poor.

I argued the fact that the union had sent its own representative to polygraph school, and that they could stop the investigation in its tracks if they could show that the officer was not lying. They decided against it. I assume because of the cost, but it left them with one more officer victim and others believing that they were in bed with the department brass.

By the way, the officer went on to another agency and submitted to a polygraph, which is required in this state for person applying for a police position, and PASSED!

I watched several careers end with allegations of misconduct, where little, if anything, was done by the union to call the city on its poor, inadequate, and sometimes unfair investigations. Many of these officers went on to other police agencies and are doing well now.

I spoke early on about us nearing a crisis in recruiting. It would make sense to me that a department would work to make its employees successful, not to fail. It also has a devastating effect on recruiting when officers themselves have been treated unfairly. I constantly hear officers — some with as little as a couple of years on the force — talking would-be recruits out of joining the department. Many suggest that the interested recruit go to the fire department, but others suggest other agencies in the state.

If your state doesn't have an officer's bill of rights as law, it should have. If you are an activist or need a cause to fight, this is a good one. The bill or statute establishes a standard such as "gross negligence" before someone can sue a police officer. Cops and their families are constantly in fear of losing what they own because of some action they have taken.

If a would-be complainant files a complaint on an officer, simply to harass or cause him harm, and could then be sued by the officer or his union, he might think twice about his actions.

Humor Behind the Badge

Most of us take this job way too seriously. I don't mean that we should be too cavalier or laugh at people in crisis, but just lightening up a little can go a long ways to calming someone down. I used humor often to defuse situations.

When I first pinned on the badge, I was as gung-ho and as serious as the next guy. I figured that I could whip my weight in wildcats, but you quickly learn that the gift of gab goes a lot further. You can't physically handle everyone, no matter what shape you are in.

There's a term known as "contempt of cop" that gets a lot of young officers in trouble. It means we told someone to do something and they didn't listen to us. Competitive spirit then kicks in, and someone has to win the conflict. Officers must learn that not everyone will yield to their authority, and they have to have a backup plan if a lawful order doesn't work.

I hadn't been an officer for more than six months when I encountered my first dumb crook, someone who didn't play by the rules. I was patrolling a small town when I was flagged down by a young man who asked me for directions. I gave him the directions, and as he went to the car, he said, "Oh, by the way, I just stole this car." He then drove off recklessly.

Once I collected my wits, I was in pursuit. I chased him for several miles into a state woodland area alone, and when I crested a hill, I saw him parked in the roadway, waiting for me. I was in pretty good shape back then, and the fight was on. Backup was coming from miles away, but I managed somehow to prevail. When the first state troopers showed up, they spent a considerable amount of time collecting what was left of my uniform.

I later learned that this was a local mentally ill person who was just bored and wanted some excitement.

Yet another encounter with a dumb crook and a funny moment for me happened when we were at a large shopping mall, setting up for a crime prevention fair. Police cars from several agencies, bomb squad displays, and K9 units, along with a couple dozen officers were in the mall. I was contacted by a loss prevention agent from one of the department stores, who told me they were watching a suspected shoplifter who was grabbing expensive leather jackets from the displays without any concern for sizes.

The agent suspected the suspect would be coming out a side door, and he was right. Within a couple of minutes, the suspect came running out, carrying armloads of leather coats. The look on his face was priceless when he saw the army of officers waiting in the parking lot.

Even being heavily outnumbered, he decided to make a run for it. He was getting a pretty good lead on us until the arrival of Phil the talking car. Phil was a 1978 Dodge Aspen patrol car set up with a public address system and a set of headlights that would flash when he spoke. Phil delivered crime prevention messages such as "don't go with strangers" or "just say no to drugs." Watching this bad guy run from this talking car hit me so funny, I was out of the race because I couldn't breathe. I was laughing too hard.

The suspect was eventually caught, and I hope that if this incident didn't at least scare him straight, that he learned the importance of casing his target and not hitting a location that is having a police convention or a crime fair.

Much later in my career, I was dispatched to a disturbance in a bar and was the first to arrive. Just after pulling into the parking lot, an obviously intoxicated male came staggering out. I approached him and asked him if he was the reason I was called. He didn't respond, and calmly walked directly to my patrol car and began urinating on the front tire of my fully marked patrol car.

Thirty years ago, if this would have happened, I would have quickly arrested this guy right after the zipper started down. Now it was all I could do not to laugh uncontrollably. I asked him if he was finished, and he nodded yes and then walked to the back seat on his own and got in. And yes, he was the reason for the call.

CAREER SURVIVAL

In the late 1990s, an assistant chief and I were discussing problem areas where officers were winding up in trouble, whether the officers' actions were misconduct, use-of-force issues, driving of a city vehicle, or general conduct that would not have been a problem when they were a civilian. It was decided that I would develop a "Career Survival" plan to see if we could aid these young officers with staying out of trouble.

We felt that if it came from a more senior officer and also one who was a union representative, the young officers might listen a little closer than if the message was delivered by an instructor in the academy or by "management."

I developed the program, which is still in use by the agency today, as well as other agencies that requested a copy of our training outline.

I spoke earlier in the book about citizens who get the knowledge about police work from the movies, but unfortunately, so do many police officers. We often have to call someone down on their behavior for something that they did or said, that could later be traced back to the movies. "Go ahead, make my day" is a repeat offender. The movie *Choir Boys* about officers who drank too much and fired their guns for the fun of it is also one that I believe some young troops have tried to copy.

Often, the officers we get are either right out of college or chose a career change and are in their early twenties. Only last year, they were out partying with their friends and hopefully making some good choices. The choice by a young person to use "recreational drugs" is one that has destroyed the dreams of many a potential police officer.

Departments can sometimes forgive marijuana use, but never hard drugs. I know one young man who is trying desperately to get on a police department in my state, but his choice to use steroids in his college years has all but destroyed those dreams.

Police officers, especially young ones, are anxious to get to the scene and catch a bad guy or help someone in need, but often overdrive their abilities. It is important for those in training positions or senior officers to help the new troop to "manage his adrenaline." When I was a field training officer, I had a rookie driving when an emergency call was broadcast. We were racing down the street when I asked him where we were going. He properly responded by saying "to a robbery in progress"; the only problem was that we were going in the exact opposite direction of the call.

His adrenaline was so high that he just started driving, not knowing where to. I had to take us out of the game for a couple of minutes while I calmed him down. Managing one's adrenaline is also important when it comes to using force, especially if it followed a stressful pursuit.

After an officer drives at dangerous speeds, with the siren blaring for some distance, endangering himself and others, that adrenaline could conceivably wind up causing the officer to drag the suspect through a car window (usually open) or giving a couple extra squeezes on the cuffs, if not worse. It is important that another officer, regardless of their time on the department, step in to calm down another officer who might be losing it.

I referred to it as the "tag, you're out theory." Even with more than thirty years on, I would appreciate it if another officer would tap me on the shoulder and tell me to "take a walk."

These usually aren't brutal officers or rebels; they are just troops who couldn't control themselves after their adrenaline was off the chart.

There used to be a standard saying in the old days in law enforcement that an officer could lose his career to "booze, broads, or bucks."

That is probably still true to this day, but in my thirty-plus years, I saw less than a half a dozen officers go bad when it came to taking something that didn't belong to them. Our department had too many checks and balances to allow for bribes or corruption. The booze and broads are still a problem. When you recruit from the human race, you cannot seek out only those who don't drink alcohol, and there is usually no way to determine if an officer will have an indiscretion when it comes to sexual behavior.

I used to start the misconduct section of my class by putting three letters on the blackboard. Those letters were: Z R F. I went on to explain that it was going to cost about 17 percent of them their jobs. ZRF is "Zipper Retention Failure." I could never figure it out why a young officer would work so hard to get through the academy, stay up all night shining shoes and studying, writing essays and putting up with military-style discipline, only to waste it away with a miscue with a young lady. I singled out the male troop in this area, because they were responsible for more than 90 percent of the misconduct.

One person told me that it was because it was easier for a male officer to get in trouble with "on-duty" sex because the female officer would have to get totally undressed to commit the offense. I didn't do any research on that topic, but I guess it makes sense.

Sometimes in the law enforcement career, an officer feels that the only person he can trust is another cop. This is picked up early on, either from too many bad experiences or from war stories from another, more senior officer.

The truth is that most citizens support the police. The best backup a state trooper has on a lonely stretch of the highway is a truck driver. Many state troopers or sheriff's deputies have had their bacon saved by a truck driver willing to stop and get involved.

Some truckers are so willing to help that they set up their own roadblocks to stop a fleeing suspect. That isn't always the best idea, and most police jurisdictions will discourage this because of liability concerns, but man, it's a good feeling when a citizen gets involved to help corral a bad guy. When I was a young sheriffs deputy in the '70s and a trucker helped me with an accident or an arrest, I would always see that they got a hefty supply of road flares.

If you are thinking about becoming a police officer and enjoy hurting people or were a bully in school, I would strongly recommend you seek another career, possibly playing football or being a professional bouncer. This is not the job for you.

I want an officer who feels bad after using force and hurting someone, even if it was done to protect the officer or someone else. We can deal with the officer's post-traumatic stress after using force and reassuring him that he did the right thing to survive.

I always cringe when I see an officer on television giving the "high five" to another cop after using force on a suspect. These is probably just an adrenaline release, and please consider that as such when reviewing use-of-force issues, but it still looks really bad!

My agency was sued following a use-of-force application where the suspect eventually died. The officer gave a "high five" simply because he won the encounter, not knowing that the suspect would later die of complications. The officer was eventually charged and tried, but won in a court of law. The "high five" celebration became a point of contention for the plaintiff's attorney, implying that the cop enjoyed the outcome.

I personally knew that officer, and also knew how the end results nearly destroyed his life.

12 WAYS TO HAVE A LASTING CAREER

1. Always be truthful. Report writing, investigations, and testifying in court.

2. Use only that force which is reasonable and necessary. (Manage your adrenaline.)

3. Don't let situations become personal. Walk away, if it can be done safely, and let someone else deal with the bad guy.

4. Treat everyone, including the suspects, the way you would want another officer to treat your family.

5. Remember that driving is the number-one cause of discipline, civil action, and injury to an officer.

6. Engage your brain before depressing the gas pedal; speeding may not be warranted.

7. Don't overextend yourself financially.

8. Don't be a twenty-four-hour cop. Take police action only in a felony or serious matter.

9. Remember that your personal life is now a concern to the department and the community. If you drink, set a reasonable limit or have a designated driver. DUI can cost you your job.

10. Remember, it is not "us against them." Most citizens appreciate and support the police.

11. Remember, you are in uniform. Watch what you do and say in public (restaurants, etc.).

12. Remember, this job should be color blind. Provide equal service to ALL.

ABOUT THE AUTHOR

Bryan Muth is a thirty-four-year veteran of law enforcement and recently retired from one of the country's largest police departments. He is a past representative for a large police union and has taught "career survival" to hundreds of rookie cops.

Printed in the United States
75618LV00006B/373-423

9 781420 888768